RHINO!

Written by Eduard Zingg

Published by Abdo & Daughters, 6535 Cecilia Circle, Edina, Minnesota 55439

Copyright © 1993 by World Wild Life Films (Pty.) Limited, Postfach 6586, 8023 Zurich, Switzerland

Edited By: Jim Abdo and Bob Italia for Abdo & Daughters Publishing

Text and Photographs: Eduard Zingg
Illustrations and Maps: W. Michel and K. Wozniak

International copyrights reserved in all countries. No part of this book may be reproduced without written permission from the copyright holder. Printed in the U.S.A.

Library of Congress Cataloging-in-Publication Data

Zingg, Eduard, 1940-
    Rhino / written by Eduard Zingg; [edited by Bob Italia].
       p.   cm. -- (An African animal adventure)
    Includes index.
    Summary: The author recounts his experiences on an expedition in the Kalahari region of Botswana and describes some of the different animals found there.
    ISBN 1-56239-219-0
    1. Zoology -- Botswana -- Juvenile literature.   2. Black rhinoceros -- Botswana -- Juvenile literature.   3. White rhinoceros -- Botswana -- Juvenile literature.   4. San (African people) -- Juvenile literature.
[1. Zoology -- Botswana.   2. Botswana -- Description and travel.]
I. Italia, Robert, 1955-   .   II. Title.   III. Series: Zingg, Eduard, 1940- African animal adventure.
QL337.B68Z565   1993
599.72'8 -- dc20   93-7602
                                                                CIP
                                                                 AC

Table of Contents

The Rhinoceros 4

The Wildebeest 10

Looking for Lions 13

The African Hyena 17

The Aardwolf 23

The Kalahari Bushmen 25

The Eland 28

The African Ostrich 31

The Chameleon 33

Victoria Falls 35

Glossary 37

Index 40

Before us now lay the Kalahari Desert. It covers almost two-thirds of the country of Botswana. It has long sand dunes, constantly changing in shape and size. There is also acacia thorn bush and scrub bush— a sparse woodland without surface water. About once a year a little rain falls, turning the dry, sandy land into a temporary colorful carpet of flowers and greenery.

THE RHINOCEROS

The rhino follows a zig-zag course because it can't move its head from side to side. This helps it keep sight of any enemies. Despite good hearing and a good sense of smell, it often cannot make out in which direction the danger lies. Sometimes it runs right into it. It either turns at the last moment or attacks.

As both the African rhinos are actually gray in color, they are more easily distinguished by the shape of their mouth. The white rhino is square-jawed, while the black rhino has a pointed jaw, a receding chin, and an extended upper lip. This allows it to eat twigs, young bushes and saplings. The square-jawed rhino eats grass. It prefers the sweet types of grasses mainly found in the forests. Its habitat is therefore limited. This is why the white rhino is not seen far and wide like the black rhino.

A female rhinoceros will defend her young with the utmost courage. Since adult rhinos have bad eyesight, it is the calf which usually gives the warning of approaching danger.

The white rhinoceros, also known as the grass rhinoceros, is completely dependent on water. It must have water every two to four days if it is to survive.

Apart from man, the rhino has no enemies except when it is young and alone. A rhino usually meets its death fighting another rhino during mating season. It has also died in accidents caused by its weak eyesight. They fall off cliffs, get stuck between rocks, drown in flood waters, or get stuck in the mud.

The rhino turns aggressive when disturbed, as I found out for myself some years ago.

Our tents were pitched fairly close to each other in high yellow grass in a hilly area which had some thick forest nearby. My companion, Mutero, and I knew from the local inhabitants that rhinos were to be found there. They are known to be both dangerous and fast-moving.

In recent years there have been several incidents in which rhinos have impaled human beings and carried them quite a few yards. With determination we wound our way uphill and down through a valley, passing a few tribal villages. The huts were built on piles of mud and straw. As usual, Mutero and the villagers exchanged waves. Mutero shouted to them that we were looking for the *Chipembere,* as the locals called the rhino.

After awhile we stopped in a clearing in the middle of the bush. There we found what we had come to film. Two rhinos lay perfectly still, as if they had not noticed us. I set up the camera under an acacia tree. Mutero stayed with the camera as I got in the landrover to try and excite the two rhinos.

As I moved through the bush in the landrover, the crackling of the branches beneath the wheels must have disturbed the two beasts. When they jumped up, I saw that it was a mother and her calf. We were not more than 50 yards (46 meters) away when the mother lifted her head high.

Her ears turned tensely in all directions. I believed that this would be the moment when they would charge us. I hoped Mutero had the camera ready. I looked around for the best escape route when she began to charge. With her calf behind her. Suddenly both stopped, and for no apparent reason the mother changed her course. At high speed, both started running toward the acacia tree where Mutero was filming. Mutero left the camera where it was and quickly leapt into the tree. He was unlucky, because the thorns in the tree tore his hands so badly he couldn't use them for weeks.

The rhino stopped in front of the camera and stamped thunderously so that the earth seemed to shake. Then it charged the tree, sticking its horn into it. The camera was not touched. At first Mutero couldn't stop laughing. The rhino stood still with its ears twitching. I tried to distract it by bringing the landrover nearer to it. But it turned its back to us and ran towards a nearby river, vanishing down the bank. The calf followed. I drove the landrover directly under the tree so Mutero could jump on top of it. His hands were bleeding and his clothes were torn to shreds.

This experience taught me that rhinos are unpredictable and behave differently than you may expect. The camera and the landrover were still intact, and the adventure had a happy ending.

At 5 o'clock in the morning, a roar awakened us. It was repeated a few times, coming nearer and nearer. I dozed off again until there was another roar, this time very close. I grabbed my rifle and looked out. There it stood, less than 300 feet (91 meters) away, an enormous Kalahari black-maned lion. Robert had not realized the danger when he first awoke.

He had popped his head out of his sleeping bag and then quickly covered up again. This last roar got him quickly to his feet, along with Peter and the two assistants. I told everyone to get into the the landrovers. I checked that my rifle was loaded and climbed on top of a truck. The lion came closer and closer. It was a huge specimen.

It stopped 100 feet (30 meters) from the trucks, then started moving towards us again. I watched it without blinking. Its eyes were riveted on me. It was old and looked restless and hungry. There were now only 45 feet (14 meters) between us, and it stood immobile as if it were laying claim to the area.

Robert slammed the door of the landrover. The lion jumped back. His mane was bristling. It looked as if he wanted to attack. His movement backwards gave me an opportunity to aim. Suddenly he crouched, ready to spring, but not facing us. I couldn't understand why he was behaving this way. He remained crouched for nearly a halfhour. The suspense was nearly killing us.

Suddenly the earth seemed to vibrate. The lion took off in a cloud of dust. I scrambled down and chased it in the truck. The second landrover followed. Through the dust we could see it tackling a wildebeest by the throat. That was what it had been after! The wildebeest had not been far from the landrover. The lion was breathing heavily. It had been a great effort for the old lion.

THE WILDEBEEST

The blue wildebeest (WILL-dah-beest) is a strangely-fashioned antelope. Its head is heavy and blunt. It has a shaggy white beard, knobby curved horns, and a sparse, stringy black mane. The bulky shoulders give way to a spindly hindquarters and a plumed tail that flicks around with a will of its own.

Horns are present in both males and females. They are curved like those of the buffalo. The bull's horns are more massive and widespread and can be 30 inches (76 centimeters) long. A full-grown bull can weigh 510 pounds (230 kilograms).

A lone wildebeest seems rather dull, but in a big herd they convey a strange beauty and power. Wildebeest herds on the march are most impressive. Trudging along in single file or several abreast, they move in a hunched walk. They only break into a gallop when they come upon a hill or valley. Their urge to stay with herd, to move in the direction of others, causes them to press forward no matter what is in their path.

I have seen a group of lions sitting under bushes watching a herd of wildebeest pass them. Within a few hours the lions had captured six wildebeest. Yet the rest of the herd rushed recklessly ahead. They wouldn't stop for their dead herd members or the smell of blood and lions.

The wildebeest calf often falls prey to the hyena. Within ten minutes of its birth the calf stumbles along, its frail body pressed to the side of its mother. With herds large and constantly on the move, a calf that becomes separated from its mother by even 70 feet (21 meters) may never see her again.

The wildebeest is numbered in the millions in southern Africa. Its ungainly appearance conceals a surprising agility and great stamina. It takes long distance journeys in search of food and water.

Cows will not accept a strange calf. A lost calf slowly dies of starvation unless attacked by a predator.

A lost youngster at first dashes back and forth, screaming loudly. But its voice is lost in the rumble of pounding hooves. It repeatedly runs up to a strange wildebeest only to be pushed away. Exhausted, the calf finally gives up. Once when we passed close to a wildebeest herd, an orphan galloped up to our landrover as if this steel body were its mother. It ran alongside the truck for several miles until sunset. Then it became so dark it vanished into the night. Calves will sometimes attach themselves to zebra and eland, walking along with the herd, quite ignored. One often sees wildebeest mingled with zebra herds.

Once in the northeast of Botswana, I stood on a hill overlooking a huge grass plain. As far as the eye could see it was covered with hundreds of wildebeest. During the rainy season, these animals live in small herds. But during the winter months (May to October) they gather in very large herds. Some of the groups are made up of only fully grown bulls. The weaker are not pushed around by the stronger ones, as is the case with some animals. Whether in small or large herds, you never see them playing with one another. When attacked by hyenas or lions, they don't try to protect or defend each other. Blue wildebeest always keep a certain distance from each other. In contrast, buffalo will move in very close to protect each other when danger approaches.

When an outsider amongst the wildebeest bulls tries to join forces with a group, they all drop their heads as if bowing to their new friend.

However, if the outsider attacks, the whole herd will gallop off into another area. They treat the area in which they live as their very own. Even if they are constantly preyed upon, they will always return.

One summer, I had not seen any lions for many days. Then one day I saw the sky thick with vultures, a living cloud that darkened the sky. There must be a predator on the hunt, I thought. The next day I decided to go on a hunt of my own with my camera.

LOOKING FOR LIONS

Mutero, my assistant, carried the film and a tripod. I had a rifle and camera around my neck. Quietly and carefully, we walked into the bush. I gestured to Mutero to move to the right while I moved to the left, circling so that we could meet at our destination. After a while, I glanced to the right and stood still as if I'd been hypnotized. There was a lion only a few yards away. He'd seen me first, and was snarling and rising to his feet. We were both startled. He stared at me with glittering eyes and a bristling mane. I kept an eye on him. But I wondered what else might be lurking in the trees or long grass. He had smelled me. The sun stood high in the sky and the sweat was pouring down my face. He had calmed down a bit, but every move I made with the rifle annoyed him. So I let the rifle hang over my shoulder and stood still. I decided that if I couldn't do anything with the rifle, I could at least try the camera. The lion was less angry when I photographed him.

For more than an hour I stood in the blazing sun. He was content in the shade of the tree. I wondered where Mutero was. Then I heard him calling me. I wondered if I should risk answering him. The lion never let me out of his sight. Mutero's calls came closer and closer. When he was within 30 yards (27 meters), the lion stood up and walked away growling and looking back until he disappeared. I was lucky, this time.

On another occasion, I was driving with friends through the bush. It was hard going, and we were only doing about 15 miles per hour (24 k/hr). The scenery was unusual, a combination of silver-gray thorn trees, tall mopani trees, and high tawny grass. After driving around in the heat for several hours we were all tired. And there were no animals in sight.

I drove on a little farther. Suddenly in the high grass to the left, getting ready to attack, was a lioness. I stopped the truck with a jerk and quickly put it in reverse. The lioness stayed where she was and ignored us. She concentrated on a water hole, where there were about thirty sable antelope. Two bulls were on watch, while the rest had their heads in the water, drinking. They made a beautiful sight, these dark-brown animals, with their black and white markings on their faces and curved horns. They appeared very calm. The lioness crouched lower in the grass so that she was hardly visible. Suddenly there was a movement within the herd, and they all looked about, sensing the danger. Slowly some of them lowered their heads to drink again. Nervously, with her muscles tensed, the lioness held her ground. Then with a quick spring she passed in front of the truck and zig-zagged towards the herd. She chose her prey, and stopped in a cloud of dust.

A well-fed lion resting after a good meal. A lion can eat up to 130 pounds (60 kilos) a day.

When the dust settled we saw the antelopes about 30 yards (27 meters) from the waterhole. Just one young beast had not been fast enough. Perhaps it was paralyzed with shock. It tried to save itself by running into the water, where it stood with its whole body quivering. The lioness never took her eyes off it. The buck started sinking into the mud and kept trying to free itself. After 20 minutes the lioness returned to the shade where she kept an eye on the buck. There she waited almost an hour. With much effort the buck tried to free itself and regain firm ground. When it reached the bank, the lioness started to chase the buck. The mud on its legs hampered the antelope. Soon our spines tingled when we heard the antelope's death cry. My friend nudged me and pointed. Six other lions had appeared. One, a powerful-looking male, stared at us. The other five were female. All the lionesses, including the killer, hung back until the male had satisfied his hunger.

Bigger animals, such as buffalo and giraffe, are generally hunted by a group of three to six lions. Even a buffalo bull has no chance of escape when one lion springs at the throat and two are on its back. Lions attack buffalo, giraffe, antelope, zebra, monkeys and baboons. They even eat large snakes, which they kill with a blow of their paw. I have seen kills at all times of the day.

The roaring can be heard far away. After the hunt, the lions start to eat. They can eat up to 130 pounds (60 kilograms) a day, one quarter of their own weight. After a good feed, they can go without food for a long time. When they have eaten their fill, they lie lazily in the shade. Even a fully-fed lion can be dangerous when disturbed.

I remember when I was driving through the bush with two landrovers. We had come across a group of lions which had just killed a giraffe. We filmed them for several hours. By then they had eaten their fill and were lying in the shade. One of my friends in the truck behind wanted to get closer to the lions with his camera. He climbed out of the back of the truck and set up his tripod. As quick as lightning, all the lions jumped up, snarling at him. The peaceful figures had suddenly turned into furiously irritated brutes. My friend fainted from shock and fell to the ground. I quickly moved my truck alongside the other, with my friend on the ground between the trucks.

The lions couldn't get between them. Keeping one eye on the lions, I got out and hauled the man back into his truck. We'd had a narrow escape.

The next morning after our experience with the old lion, I was awakened early by the howling of hyenas.

THE AFRICAN HYENA

The howl of the hyena (hi-HEE-nuh) is unmistakable, starting with a low pitch and rising to a scream. They laugh when excited, and utter a variety of grunts, chuckles, and whimpers on other occasions.

You rarely see hyenas during the day, and you tend to forget all about them. Then you hear them howl at night and remember they exist. I had almost forgotten this predator until one hot day when I was travelling through the bush. I knew that there would be one or two waterholes along the way.

They had not yet dried out because water still remained in one of the arms of the river. I came upon one of the waterholes which was a pool of muddy water. An old female spotted hyena was so busy bathing herself in the mud that she never noticed my approach. She was standing in mud up to her stomach. I could see her ears sticking out above her head, as well as her back and bushy tail. She seemed to be part of the mud pool.

I switched off the engine and watched this hyena enjoying herself in the mud. Not far from the waters edge was a tall mopani tree. Behind it was a very large antbear hole near a thick green shrub.

After waiting a while, I decided to get closer. I released the brakes so that the landrover rolled closer to the waterhole. I drew to within 20 yards (18 meters). But then the hyena suddenly jumped out of the mud and ran to the antbear hole. Then I saw why. She had made it the hideout for her young.

Two to three young are born at a time, usually in a hollow like an unused antbear hole. Sometimes two females may have pups in the same hole. The small pups are kept underground for several months. They are fed food regurgitated by their parents. You can often see hyenas walking through a field carrying a carcass which is for their underground young.

Hyenas are very powerful animals. Their jaws, teeth and muscles surpass those of larger carnivores. The hyena can crack a bone of a buffalo as one of us can crack a matchstick. They can completely demolish the largest bones of a hippo and even an elephant.

A young hyena will grow up to be a lonely scavenger, purely nocturnal and very secretive. Its search for food may take it far from its home.

Bones left lying around by other predators are chewed to bits by the hyena. The strong stomach juices can also digest skins and hooves. They watch the movements of vultures to guide them to a kill. The hyena is a scavenger, taking over when the predator has eaten its fill, or sometimes even before. I once watched a pack of eight hyenas chase a lioness from her kill, leaving her no choice but to abandon her prey.

One of the most interesting characteristics of the hyena is its very sensitive ears. They can hear the calls of vultures, wild dogs, and lions from hundreds of feet away.

In African superstition, the hyena ranks high. It is closely connected with witches. It is said that witches ride on the backs of hyenas, and that witches turn into hyenas so they can hunt. The tail, ears and whiskers of the hyena are valued by the witchdoctors. In parts of Africa, hyenas are regarded as natural undertakers. The dead are left out to be disposed by them.

In the meantime, the sun had turned a fiery red and was about to set on the horizon. The time passed so quickly that I realized it was too late to return to camp. This did not disturb me too much. I opened a tin of food, pulled out a blanket and went to sleep in the landrover. As I was about to settle down to sleep I heard strange noises nearby. I looked out the back of the truck and saw the hyena mother, with her plump, dirty body coming closer. Her nose seemed to be split, her ears were torn, and her eyes looked glassy. Her snout was slashed so that it looked as if she was hissing. She looked so thin that I felt sorry for her and her little family.

It looked as if this old mother (I guessed she was about 10 years old) had put up many a fight for existence.

Without noticing me, she passed about five yards away. It looked as if she was looking for food. She was in no shape for hunting. But as a mother, she had no choice. With a sudden howl, she vanished into the bush. The moon was full but I lost sight of her.

In the middle of the night, I was awakened by a howl such as I have never heard before or since. It sounded like the death cry of a young antelope. Not knowing what it was, I fell asleep again, and didn't awake until the next morning.

On a dead tree trunk near the waterhole, where well-fed vultures kept watch, the hyena lay sunning herself with a full stomach. It was obvious that she had enjoyed a good meal the night before and was digesting it.

Hyenas mostly live off the kills of other predators. They can reach a speed of 30 miles/hr (48 k/hr). Hyenas also bring down their prey by attacking sensitive spots. They share their prey with one another. But it is not a peaceful meal. The urge for food makes them snappish and ill-tempered. No wonder that with the crowding and pushing, cannibalism occurs. They bite each other's ears, noses, and paws.

During the day you never see more than two to three hyenas together. But during the night they hunt in large packs. They eat on the spot rather than dragging provisions to their homes. Their cousin, the brown hyena, does drag the prey to its home. Brown hyenas are strictly nocturnal, and rarely seen at all.

Spotted hyenas stand about 3 feet (.9 meters) high at the shoulder, from which the body slopes sharply downwards. They are nearly 6 feet (1.8 meters) long from nose to the tip of their tails. They weigh about 190 pounds (85 kilograms). The males are smaller than the females. They have rounded ears and a gray to reddish color with irregular spots. The front of the face and lower limbs are blackish. Hyena pups are ruled by their mother more than by the father.

Hyenas are unattractive beasts. They are both cowardly and aggressive, and they will attack any animal which is injured or small. To protect it from hyenas, a rhinoceros mother will keep her newborn calf hidden in thick bush until it is about two months old. At this age the calf is large enough so that it has a fairly good chance of survival, as long as it stays near its mother. I once saw a rhinoceros mother crossing a clearing in a forest, followed by twelve hyenas. All the animals vanished into the woods. Two hours later, I found them again. As I got closer to the rhino mother and her calf, I saw that the little one was wounded. The mother had been successful in defending her young. But the hyenas continued to attack. I decided to separate the hyenas from the rhinos by driving my landrover between them until the hyenas were frightened off.

Hyenas will eat anything, and what they don't eat they will chew to bits. Often in camp, the hyenas would chew on the tires of the trucks and tear apart the laundry. At night, hyenas can be more dangerous than the lions.

THE AARDWOLF

I was also lucky enough to photograph an aardwolf (ARD-wulf) one day. The aardwolf is another strange mammal of Africa. It is much like the hyena. It lives in the scrubby bush country or in open sandy plains. It is a very shy creature. At first glance this creature may look like a jackal. But its coat is much rougher, and it has a smaller head. Unfortunately, its timid nature seldom permits it to be seen for any length of time.

The aardwolf has very small, weak teeth. It eats insects, worms and flying ants as well as eggs. Its weak jaws prevent it from killing its own prey. It is a scavenger, eating leftovers.

The aardwolf is a pale, sandy color. It has dark vertical stripes on its sides. Its heavy mane has long buff-colored hairs with black tips along the back. The ears are narrow, fairly long and pointed. The face below the eyes is black. The aardwolf has four toes on the hind feet and five on the front.

Shoulder height is about 20 inches (51 centimeters). Length is 35 inches (89 centimeters) and it has a long bushy tail of which the bottom half is black. It weighs about 22 pounds (10 kilograms).

Two to three young are born in an underground burrow. The young are colored like the adults.

When attacked, the aardwolf raises its heavy mane into a striking position. This way it looks twice its real size. It then ejects a musky smell much like a skunk. Its enemies usually don't like this smell. Because of its clumsy and slow movements, it is often caught by predators.

The aardwolf is pale, sandy in color, and marked with vertical dark brown stripes on its sides.

The miraculous thing about the Kalahari is that it is a desert only in the sense that it contains no surface water. Otherwise its deep fertile sands are covered with grass. It has, in places, thick bush and clumps of trees. They are filled with their own variety of game— all kinds of birds, lions and leopards. When the rains come, it grows sweet-tasting grasses, and many edible wild fruits which are put to use by the Kalahari Bushmen.

THE KALAHARI BUSHMEN

As prehistoric human survivors, the Bushmen present a unique phenomenon. They are pale brown and small, never reaching a height more than 5 feet (1.5 meters). The Bushman's color is unlike that of the other peoples of Africa. A remarkable thing is that his skin never burns in the hot sun. The shape of his face is mongoloid, with small eyes slightly slanted. His eyes are deep brown, a color that is hardly ever seen except in antelope. He can see things at such a distance that his powers of vision have become a legend in Africa. To tell you how good the Bushman's eyesight is, Mutero and I once saw a bee hovering nearby, as did a Bushman who was with us. The bee moved off, and disappeared from our view. But the Bushman could still see it. He followed the bee for sometime. Strangly enough the tsetse-fly and the mosquito do not seem to bother the Bushmen. Perhaps its the scent they emit. At any rate the Bushmen are hardly ever bitten by insects.

In good hunting times, the Bushmen eat so much that they often look pregnant. This slows them down dangerously when wild animals are around. When they are slim there is almost no person to match their speed.

The Kalahari Bushman is self-reliant, resourceful, unafraid of man, beast, or opinion, and generous, with a boundless capacity of endurance.

The Bushmen live in conditions which to us seem impossible for existence. They have special talents and gifts which enable them to survive. The Bushmen can find water where no one else can. They sink a reed into the earth and suck up underground water. Otherwise they dig out wild plants which contain water.

The nomadic Bushman always returns to his own territory. But he roams far and wide in areas where he can find water. The water they suck up is stored in empty ostrich eggs, which are then buried at strategic places for future use. They make use of all available vegetation, and know more than a hundred varieties of edible plants.

The Bushmen are self-reliant, resourceful, and unafraid of man, or beast. Bushmen are also generous with a boundless capacity of endurance. Above all else they are hunters. The women and children dig the earth with their sticks for edible roots. In the season they harvest the bush for berries and other wild fruits. Their lives and happiness depend mainly on the meat provided by the men. They live on what they hunt in areas where there is no contact with other forms of humanity. To get his meat, the Bushman kills with a bow and arrow. He is a very skilled hunter. A Bushman bow is effective at about 492 feet (150 meters). Originally the arrowheads were made of bone or flint. But they are now made of iron. The arrowheads are dipped in poison made from insect larvae, roots, and reptiles. A stronger poison is used for lions and leopards. These deadly mixtures are made with great care. The Bushman always carries them in a pouch. He also carries a snake-bite cure.

The Bushman hunter is so skillful that he will match himself against the meanest animals in the bush. It is said that he will provoke a male elephant by darting in and out of the herd. He will rely on his knowledge of the elephant and his own speed to survive. He does this until the angry elephant charges him. Then twisting and turning, and uttering magic words with a shriek, the Bushman will flee until the animal starts to chase him. Then a companion Bushman will run up behind to attack the only place where such a rampant animal is vulnerable to Stone-Age weapons. He will slice through the tendons above the heel, making the elephant fall helplessly. The Bushmen will then close in to attack with spears and knives.

Giraffes are also caught by Bushmen. They are not as easy to hunt as it might seem. Due to their height, they can see far away. They are also very fast. I once tried to catch a baby giraffe in my landrover. There was no sign of parents at first, but suddenly the mother appeared. She chased me, and I was lucky to get away.

The eland is the Bushman's favorite meat. He uses a special poison on the tip of his arrow for them. The poison does not circulate in the body and does not spoil the meat. Bushmen always aim for the heart.

THE ELAND

The eland (E-land) is the largest and heaviest of all antelopes, a very bulky animal about the size of a domestic cattle. At the shoulder it measures 6 feet (1.8 meters), and the length is 9 feet (2.7 meters). It can weigh up to 2,000 pounds (900 kilograms). The females are somewhat smaller.

The eland is the largest and heaviest of all antelopes, a very bulky animal, about the size of domestic cattle.

Eland have many things in common with cattle. The shoulders are humped, and a dewlap extends from the throat to the chest. The tail is long and slender. The color is reddish-brown. The older bulls have gray colors interspersed. The horns spiral widely backwards, ending in straight points. They are heavier in the bulls and slimmer in the cows.

Eland eat leaves, wild fruits, as well as shoots and pods. A herd usually consists of 25 to 30 animals of various ages. They roam far and wide. At one time, they were found on the large open plains of southern Africa. Nowadays they are confined to game reserves, and the western and northern parts of Africa.

Their size is misleading; eland are very graceful. They can jump over barriers as high as 7 feet (2.1 meters). Although shyer than most antelope, eland will sometimes mingle with other varieties and with zebra. They are extremely gentle. They do not fight among themselves, and they seldom charge their attackers even when wounded or cornered. The only sound they utter is a grunt. Eland can maintain themselves with little food. They can also go for long periods with little water.

The eland's main enemy is the lion. The females and young are sometimes dragged down by packs of wild dogs, or may fall prey to leopards. Poachers often go after eland, not for trophies as is usually the case, but because of their tasty meat.

We often think of the ostrich as a stupid bird, with a reputation for burying its head in the sand. But what I experienced is that in battle for survival the ostrich is as brave as any predator.

THE AFRICAN OSTRICH

One evening, just before sunset, the male and female were pecking at the dry ground. Their chicks were running around at their feet. Suddenly, a young lioness appeared. She was on her own and inexperienced at hunting. She stalked the family for sometime. She suddenly jumped from the bush and sent the ostriches into a panic. She then snatched one of the chicks into her jaws. The lioness dropped her dead prey and went after more. Hampered by the slowness of the chicks, the normally swift ostriches could not escape quickly enough. Realizing the danger his family was in, the male ostrich attacked in a move that surprised the lioness.

Spitting, wings flapping, and feet kicking, the male ostrich battled the lioness while the female and chicks ran for safety into the bush. The lioness backed away. Seizing this opportunity, the ostrich ran away from the bush. Although he had a good start his chances of getting away seemed slim. But running at a speed of 44 miles/hour (70 k/hr), he made it.

A full-grown ostrich is more than 6 feet (1.8 meters) tall and weighs up to 288 pounds (130 kilograms). The female is smaller. The ostrich likes the summer and winter for its most vigorous activity: mating and nesting.

A great wanderer in search of food and water, the ostrich will eat almost anything. Though it is chiefly a browser on shrubs and plants, it loves to pick up and swallow small bright objects.

THE CHAMELEON

The chameleon (kuh-MEE-lee-un) has the shape of a prehistoric animal. It looks like a miniature dragon, with scaly tail, hard skin, and a ridged back. The soft fat of its hands and feet almost hide its claws. Its mouth is wide like a frog's. The eyes are mounted at the tips of movable cones. They can move independently of each other. It can look in different directions with each eye. It will focus both of them on an insect that it is going to attack. Insects are caught with the tongue which can be shot out to a length of 6 inches (15 centimeters) in a fraction of a second. It picks up the insect and drags it back to be swallowed.

When frightened, this little creature will open its mouth and appear to be sucking in great amounts of air. The Africans believe that it lives off of air. Its body will swell rapidly until the skin seems as if it is going to burst. Its whole frame will tremble as if preparing for violent action.

A chameleon moves very slowly. The hand of one frontlimb will tighten its grip of the branch on which it has been lying. At the same time, the other hand seems to slacken its hold. The tail, which will have been curved around the branch like a spring, will slowly straighten.

The chameleon is a bush-dwelling lizard. Its true habitat is up among the branches and leaves. Its feet, with toes at 180 degrees in groups of two and three, are specially adapted for getting a firm hold on branches and twigs. It is never in a hurry. Whether it is up in the trees or on the ground, the chameleon moves with a hesitating stride. It takes seconds to advance one leg, then sways back and forth several times as if wondering whether to complete the next step.

Most Africans have a superstitious fear of chameleons, which in fact are completely harmless. Their ability to change color is more limited than once was thought. But most chameleons are dark-colored in the early morning, to absorb heat from the sun.

Normally the chameleon's body is flattened vertically, like a fish. But in anger or fright, it puffs itself up and arches its back in a frightening display. At the same time, the yellow throat pouch swells, and the body color becomes almost black. It then snaps and hisses viciously, all bluff, for it cannot even nip a finger severely. But often the bluff scares its enemies. The color of this reptile changes as the light alters, sometimes being quite different on each side of the body. In darkness it is primrose yellow. In light it assumes a variety of greens, yellows and browns, with a little blue.

VICTORIA FALLS

We had breakfast at the edge of Victoria Falls. Its cascades were right in front of us. Victoria Falls are the second biggest falls in the world. The water falls 430 feet (131 meters) into the chasm. Water sprays up to keep the surrounding vegetation green all year long.

"Scenes so lovely must have been gazed upon by angels in their flight." So wrote David Livingstone, the Scottish missionary-explorer, when he discovered the Victoria Falls on 16th November, 1855. He was overwhelmed by the beauty and magnitude of the scene as he gazed at the huge volume of water plunging into the gorge and rising again in great columns of misty fury. When the Zambesi River reaches its peak volume, some six hundred and twenty million gallons of water plummet over the falls. Columns of spray rising up 400 yards (365 meters), looking like the smoke of a huge field fire, visible up to some 50 miles (80 kilometers) away. The local inhabitants call the Victoria Falls "Mosi oa tunya," meaning "the smoke that thunders."

The local inhabitants call Victoria Falls "the smoke that thunders."

The time of year was great for taking photos. The water was just at the right level. Robert and Peter took the opportunity of recording the thunderous noise of the falls. Highly satisfied, we returned with our cameras to have lunch, our last meal together under the blue African sky.

Towards evening we covered the last few miles into Livingstone. For the first time in three months we saw flashing advertisements and street lights. The traffic flowed through the streets. We were back in the middle of civilization. Although we were happy, healthy, and unhurt, our thoughts went back to Botswana, a land where nature has stayed unspoiled, a land where people survive by the most primitive methods, where animals follow their cycle of hunger, thirst, fighting for survival, and caring for their young. With much exertion, we had experienced this land.

GLOSSARY

Acacia Tree - a tree from which gum is obtained.

Africa - a continent (large body of land) south of the Mediterranean Sea between the Atlantic and Indian Ocean.

Baboon - a large African monkey.

Botswana - a country in southeastern Africa.

Bushman - a member of an aboriginal tribe of southern Africa.

Chameleon - a small lizard that can change color according to its surroundings.

Carnivore - a meat-eating animal.

Eland - an antelope-type animal.

Expedition - a journey for a particular purpose.

Hippopotamus - a large African river animal with tusks, short legs, and thick skin.

Hyena - a flesh-eating animal with a howl that sounds like wild laughter.

Inhabitant - one who lives in or dwells in a place.

Insect larvae - an insect in its first stage of life after coming out of the egg.

Kalahari Desert - a dry and arid region of the country of Botswana in southern Africa.

Legend - a story (true or not) handed down from the past.

Lioness - a female lion.

Mammal - a member of the class of animals that raise their young on mothers milk.

Mane - long hair on an animals neck (lion, horse).

Mongoloid - people resembling the mongols, with broad flat faces, straight black hair, and yellowish skin.

Nomadic - people who roam from place to place; a wanderer.

Ostrich - a swift-running African bird that cannot fly and buries its head in the sand.

Predator - an animal that preys upon others.

Prehistoric - of ancient period, before written records.

Prey - an animal that is hunted or killed by another for food.

Primitive - early stage of civilization.

Provisions - providing resources for future need.

Reptiles - cold-blooded animals with a backbone, short legs or no legs; lizard.

Rhinoceros - a large thick-skinned animal of Africa.

Sable - a large antelope-like animal.

Scavenger - animals who search for decaying flesh for food.

Specimen - a part or individual taken as an example of the whole.

Stone Age - early period of civilization when weapons and tools were made of stone and not metal.

Tsetse fly - a tropical African fly that carries and transmits disease (sleeping sickness) through its bite.

Victoria Falls - a waterfall in Botswana, Africa.

Vulture - large bird of prey that lives on the flesh of dead animals.

Wildebeest - an ox-like animal or gnu.

Zambesi River - a river in Botswana, Africa.

Zebra - an African animal of the horse family with a body covered with black and white stripes.

INDEX:
Aardwolf - 23
Antbear - 18
Antelope - 14, 16, 25, 28
Botswana - 4, 12, 13
Bushmen - 25, 27, 28
Chameleon - 33, 35
Eland - 12, 28, 30
Elephant - 18, 28
Giraffe - 16, 17, 28
Hyena - 17, 18, 20-22
Kalahari Desert - 4, 8, 21, 25
Lion - 8, 9, 12, 13, 14, 16, 17, 30, 31
Ostrich - 31
Rhinoceros - 4, 7, 8
Victoria Falls - 35
Wildebeest - 9, 10, 12
Wild dogs - 30
Zebra - 12, 16, 30

WITHDRAWN
No longer the property of the
Boston Public Library.
Sale of this material benefits the Library.